HRJC

Published by Creative Education
123 South Broad Street, Mankato, Minnesota 56001
Creative Education is an imprint of The Creative Company

Art direction by Rita Marshall
Production design by The Design Lab

Photographs by Steven J. Brown, Bruce Carr, Corbis (Archivo Iconografico, Bettmann,
Edward S. Curtis, Hulton-Deutsch, C.E. Kelly, David Lees), Cunard, Herbert L. Gatewood,
Anne Gordon, Hulton Archive, Derk R. Kuyper, Sally McCrae Kuyper, North Wind Picture
Archives (N.C. Wyeth), D. Jeanene Tiner, John Wilson

Library of Congress Cataloging-in-Publication Data

Tiner, John Hudson, 1944–
Ships & boats / by John Hudson Tiner.
p. cm. — (Let's investigate)
Summary: An introduction to the history of transportation on
the water and to various ships and watercraft.
ISBN 1-58341-257-3
1. Boats and boating—Juvenile literature. 2. Ships—Juvenile literature.
[1. Boats and boating. 2. Ships.] I. Title. II. Series.
VM150 .T55   2003
623.8'2—dc21   2002031489

First edition

2 4 6 8 9 7 5 3 1

SHIPS & BOATS

JOHN HUDSON TINER

Creative Education

SHIP & BOAT
HISTORY

Native Americans made canoes using a wooden frame covered by tree bark. Birch bark canoes were strong but light and easy to carry.

Above, a canoe
Right, boats are among the oldest forms of transportation

Earth is a planet of water. Oceans cover 71 percent of its surface, and rivers flow into the oceans from regions far inland. Because waterways are so abundant, it was a great achievement when humans first learned to build rafts, **dugouts**, and boats. Travel by water became so important that the first great cities rose up along the shores of rivers, lakes, and seas.

SHIP & BOAT

BALANCE

People of the Pacific Islands fished from the ocean in outrigger canoes. Outriggers were extra floats attached far out on one side that kept the canoes from tipping over.

5

SHIP & BOAT
STORY

THE FIRST SAILORS

Egypt, on the Nile River, became one of the world's first great nations. Drawings from as early as 4000 B.C. depict Egyptian boats. The first ones were made of bundles of papyrus, a lightweight reed that grew along the Nile. Fishermen in reed boats fished in shallow water along the riverbank. Later, wooden ships hauled grain along the Nile. The river's current carried the ships downstream. After unloading their cargo, the ships raised tall sails to catch a breeze and sail back upstream.

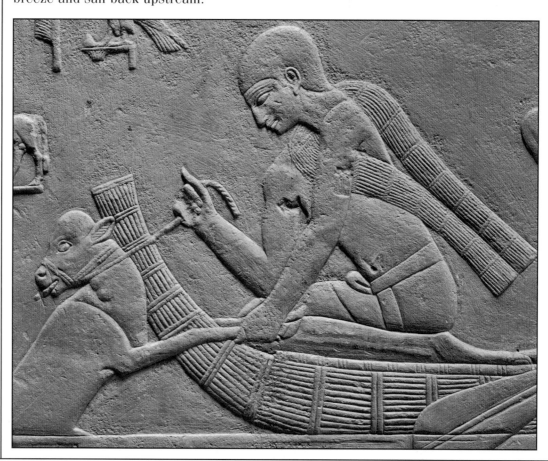

A 4,000-year-old engraving of Egyptians moving livestock across a river

7

When the wind failed, sailors depended on human muscle to propel their ships. Small Egyptian vessels carried crews of 20 rowing oarsmen. Larger ships needed as many as 200 oarsmen. Those in back used their oars to guide the ship in the right direction. Later, the addition of a larger oar called a **rudder** gave sailors greater control of their ships.

An engraving of a Phoenician vessel with rows of oarsmen

SHIP & BOAT

PASSAGE

The Mediterranean Sea opens to the Atlantic Ocean through the narrow Strait of Gibraltar. In ancient times, the strait was known as the Pillars of Hercules.

SHIP & BOAT

CHALLENGE

In 1970, Norwegian explorer Thor Heyerdahl sailed more than 3,000 miles (4,800 km) from Africa to Barbados, an island near South America, on Ra II, a boat modeled after Egyptian reed ships.

Traversed by the first great sailors, the Mediterranean Sea had many ports

Skilled early sailors such as the Greeks, Romans, and **Phoenicians** generally stayed within the Mediterranean Sea. Unlike the great oceans, this sea had predictable winds, small tides, and gentle currents. Sailors stayed close to the coast. A fear of unknown perils in the open sea kept them from sailing out of sight of land.

SAILING THE OCEANS

About A.D. 800, the Vikings, or Norsemen, of **Scandinavia** built long, narrow ships propelled by both oars and sails. Once out to sea, they raised a single sail to catch the wind. These fearless and hardy sailors crossed the stormy North Atlantic to Newfoundland, an area along the northern coast of the North American continent.

SHIP & BOAT
N A M E

Viking explorer Leif Ericson landed at Newfoundland in A.D. 1000. He called it Vinland because of the grapevines growing there.

Above, Leif Ericson in a landing boat
Left, a Viking ship on the North Atlantic

SHIP & BOAT

DISCOVERY

From 1804 to 1806, the Meriwether Lewis and William Clark expedition explored the north-west part of America and traveled to the Pacific Ocean on the Missouri, Snake, and Columbia Rivers.

By 1400, sailors had learned to sail into the wind. They sailed first to the right and then to the left. This zigzag course, called tacking, carried them forward despite a contrary wind. As sailors learned to make better use of the wind, shipbuilders did away with oars and depended on sails alone. Also in the 1400s, **navigators** began charting trustworthy air currents across the ocean. They found that, on either side of the **equator**, the **trade winds** blew east to west at a steady 12 miles (19 km) per hour. Farther north, prevailing winds blew west to east.

Sailors crossing the ocean in the 1400s relied on basic navigational tools

SHIP & BOAT
R I G H T

Starboard is the right side of a boat as one faces forward. The name came from the rudder, or steer board, that hung from the right side of ships.

SHIP & BOAT
L E F T

Port is the left side of a ship as one faces forward. A port is also a place where ships tie to a dock to load and unload passengers and cargo.

A replica of the Santa Maria, the ship that carried Columbus to the New World

In the late 1400s, European merchants looked for a sea route to India and China. In an effort to trade for oriental silk and spices, Christopher Columbus explored west to find a route to China. On August 3, 1492, he left Spain with a crew on three ships: the *Santa Maria, Nina,* and *Piñta.* The *Santa Maria* was 117 feet (36 m) long. The other two were only 50 feet (15 m) long. On October 12, he landed on an island that he named San Salvador. Instead of arriving on the rich shore of China, Columbus had arrived at the **New World**.

SHIP & BOAT
FLEET

12

Sailors discovered that there was no easy route to China. Ships sailing west had to sail around Cape Horn, the southern tip of South America. Sailing around Cape Horn was one of the most dangerous challenges seamen could face. Giant waves, stinging sea spray, and fierce winds all tested sailors' ability and courage. The trip to China and back by this route took about three years. Ships sailing east had to sail around the southern tip of Africa and across the Indian Ocean. Voyages to China by this route took about two years.

The vast distances across oceans demanded faster ships. In the 1700s, builders began adding more sails to ships and built slender, V-shaped **hulls** that cut through the water with less drag. The fastest of these ships were called clipper ships and had extra-tall **masts** that held a great expanse of sail. Clippers carried light, expensive cargo such as mail and spices. In 1851, an American clipper ship called the *Flying Cloud* sailed from New York to San Francisco in just 89 short days.

SHIP & BOAT
VOYAGE

In 1519, Spanish sea captain Ferdinand Magellan began the first voyage around the world. Of his five sailing ships and 280 sailors, only one ship and 18 crew members completed the historic journey.

Above, famed explorer Ferdinand Magellan

SHIP & BOAT
S I Z E

What's the difference between a boat and a ship? People do not agree on a firm definition, but most boats are less than 65 feet (20 m) long and cannot cross the ocean.

With their tall, sturdy masts and sails, windjammers were heavy-duty vessels

To haul heavier cargo, sailors began building windjammers, which were twice as large as clipper ships. Windjammers had four masts that rose about 150 feet (46 m) above the deck. The masts held 34 sails with a combined 45,000 square feet (4,200 sq m) of surface area to catch the wind. Windjammers hauled heavy loads such as coal, fertilizer, grain, and timber.

INLAND SAILING

Ships and boats used to traverse inland waterways looked much different than vessels built for travel over the ocean. In the 1700s and early 1800s, pioneers from the American colonies traveled west by flatboat. These boats had large, wide bottoms designed to float on shallow rivers. Flatboats simply drifted downstream with the current.

American pioneer families who traveled by flatboat lived in a cabin on the boat. When they reached their homestead, the cabin became a temporary shelter as they built a home.

15

Above, an 18th-century fur trader's boat
Left, a flatboat loaded with pioneers and livestock

SHIP & BOAT

WANDERERS

Tramp steamers are ships that have no set schedule or cargo. Instead, they go wherever business takes them. Usually they haul grain, ore, or coal.

A team of horses towing a boat along the Erie Canal in the mid-1800s

Long, narrow boats called keelboats carried passengers and cargo upstream. Keelboat operators overcame the current with punting poles—long poles that reached the bottom of the river. By pressing against the poles and walking toward the **stern**, operators pushed the boats forward. It was hard work.

Throughout the history of boating, canals have been dug to make water transportation possible where there are no rivers. In the United States, the Erie Canal was built to

connect the Hudson River to Lake Erie. This waterway, completed in 1825, was 340 miles (547 km) long. Special canal boats were built to navigate the narrow channels. Mules or horses plodding on towpaths on the shore pulled the boats along.

17

SHIP & BOAT
TRAVEL

Before the Suez Canal was dug, passengers traveling from Europe to India traveled by riverboat down the Nile and over land by camel to the Red Sea. Then they boarded a steamship to India.

A ship sailing across Egypt on the Suez Canal in the 1880s

Canals were also dug as shortcuts for ocean-going ships. The Suez Canal, completed in 1869, connected the Mediterranean Sea to the Red Sea. The completion of this canal meant that ships no longer had to sail around Africa to reach India. The Panama Canal, completed in 1914, connected the Atlantic and Pacific Oceans. This canal cut across a narrow body of land in Central America. Ships took the canal to shorten their sailing distance and avoid the dangers of Cape Horn.

STEAM-POWERED SHIPS

Boats were at the mercy of winds and currents until the early 1800s. Then the invention of the steam engine changed the world of sailing. Scottish inventor James Watt built reliable steam engines in 1775, and people with imagination soon sought to propel ships with steam power.

The steam engine, invented by James Watt (top), changed sailing forever

SHIP & BOAT
WRITING

Mark Twain, the American writer of the book Tom Sawyer, *was a riverboat pilot. He wrote about his adventures in the book* Life on the Mississippi.

SHIP & BOAT
WEIGHT

Ships and boats float because they shove aside, or displace, an amount of water equal to their weight. Weight, rather than length, is often used to describe the size of a boat.

SHIP & BOAT
STEAMING

The first steam vessel to try to cross the Atlantic Ocean was the American ship Savannah, *in 1819. It ran out of fuel partway across and had to complete the voyage under sail.*

At first, steamboats were slow, clumsy, and expensive to operate. American inventor Robert Fulton built the first steamboat that made money. His boat, the *Clermont*, was 150 feet (46 m) long. A steam engine turned paddlewheels at the middle of each side of the ship. In 1807, he tested the *Clermont* on the Hudson River between New York City and Albany. After he fired the boiler to generate steam, smoke rolled out of the smokestack, and the paddlewheels began turning. His ship carried 40 passengers at a speed of 4.7 miles (7.6 km) per hour.

Many large steamboats, called riverboats, were built as luxury hotels. Passengers entered a fancy lobby and walked on expensive carpet. Oil paintings and sparkling chandeliers decorated the ships' interiors. Chefs cooked elaborate meals, and maids and butlers served the passengers.

Right, illustrations of the Clermont
Far right, fine dining aboard a riverboat

SHIP & BOAT
SPEED

A ship's speed is measured in knots by a propeller turned by the water. A knot is one nautical mile (about 6,076 feet or 1,852 m) per hour.

SHIP & BOAT
DIVE

Before he built his steamboat, Robert Fulton created a submarine called the Nautilus. *In 1800, Fulton dove to a depth of 25 feet (7.6 m) as three crew members cranked a propeller by hand.*

A 19th-century advertisement for the passenger ships of the Cunard Line

At first, people doubted that a steamboat could cross an ocean. But in 1838, the steamship *Sirius* crossed the Atlantic. The trip wasn't easy, though. Near the end of the journey, part of the wooden ship had to be broken up and burned because it had run out of fuel. Two years later, a British ship owner named Samuel Cunard offered regular passenger service. The ships of his Cunard Line were also equipped with sails to assist the steam engines.

In 1620, a sailing ship called the *Mayflower* left Plymouth, England, for the New World. At only 90 feet (27 m) long, the *Mayflower* was a small ship, but 102 passengers had crowded aboard for the voyage. Finally, after 66 days on the Atlantic Ocean, the **pilgrims** came ashore near Cape Cod during a harsh winter. Despite suffering disease and other hardships, they built Plymouth Colony, Massachusetts—the first permanent settlement in New England.

SHIP & BOAT
LEGEND

The Flying Dutchman *is a legendary ghost ship. According to tales, it sailed aimlessly about the ocean while the captain played dice with the devil for his soul.*

23

A replica of the Mayflower, *the ship that carried the first pilgrims to America*

SHIP & BOAT

DOUBLE

A catamaran is a boat that has two slim hulls linked together with a sail mast between them. A catamaran is lightweight and fast but stays upright better than a single-hulled boat.

The sinking of the Titanic was one of the most stunning disasters in history

The large British luxury liner *Titanic* was a beautiful ship. It featured a double-bottom steel hull divided into 16 watertight compartments. Although experts considered the ship unsinkable, the *Titanic* never completed its first voyage. On April 14, 1912, it struck an iceberg in the North Atlantic and sank within three hours. The ship did not have enough lifeboats for the 2,200 passengers and crew, and about 1,500 people drowned.

SHIP & BOAT

APPARATUS

A hydrofoil is an underwater, winglike structure that raises the hull of a ship out of the water when it gets up speed. The drag of the water is reduced, and the ship burns less fuel.

SHIP & BOAT

SAILORS

A ship's deck hands steer, keep lookout, and dock and undock the ship. The engine crew maintains the motors and machinery. Stewards provide food and other services to the crew and passengers.

T he *Enterprise*, the world's first nuclear-powered aircraft carrier, was launched in 1961. Eight **atomic reactors** powered this U.S. Navy ship. At a length of 1,123 feet (343 m), the *Enterprise* was the longest warship ever built. Sailing along at nearly 35 miles (56 km) per hour while carrying 85 aircraft and a crew of 5,830, the carrier was essentially an airport at sea.

The aircraft carrier Enterprise was nearly the length of four football fields

SHIP & BOAT
LONGITUDE

Longitude is the distance east or west of the **Prime Meridian** in Greenwich, England. Longitude can be measured by comparing local time with the time in Greenwich.

SHIP & BOAT
LATITUDE

Latitude and longitude describe the location of a ship. Latitude is the distance above or below the equator and can be measured by observing the height of certain stars.

Many people enjoy vacationing on cruise ships such as the Queen Elizabeth 2

The passenger liner *Queen Elizabeth 2* set sail in 1969. A crew of 900 ran the ship and looked after the passengers, and the ship featured a theater, newspaper, dance floor, restaurants, and two swimming pools. The *QE2*, as it was known, was 963 feet (293 m) long and more than 100 feet (30 m) wide. The majestic cruise liner continued to carry passengers as of 2003.

Queen Elizabeth 2

CUNARD

SHIP & BOAT
C H A R T

A map designed for sailors is called a chart. It shows water depth, safe channels, the location of hazards such as sunken ships, and an outline of the shore.

Above, a chart

SHIP & BOAT

HELP

Tugboats are small but powerful water-craft that tow or push barges and large ships. They also help large ships dock safely.

Above, a tugboat
Right, ships may enter a harbor (top) or anchor offshore (bottom)

SPECIAL-PURPOSE SHIPS

Ships and boats are built to suit various kinds of work. Large fishing boats have freezers aboard to keep fish fresh so that fishermen can stay at sea longer. Supertankers carry crude oil and are the largest ships afloat—as long as four football fields put end to end. Their size prevents them from docking, so they anchor offshore and pump the oil to land through underwater pipelines. Container ships carry cargo in aluminum storage lockers 20 feet (6 m) long.

After the ships dock at a port, the containers are loaded onto trucks or railroad flatcars to be hauled to their final destinations.

Many sports enthusiasts enjoy old-fashioned means of boating. Each year, sailing yachts enter such races as the America's Cup. Olympic athletes compete in rowing contests, rubber rafts carry people down rivers filled with rapids, and nature lovers explore remote lakes and rivers in canoes and kayaks.

SHIP & BOAT
HANDLING

A supertanker is so large that it needs several miles to change course. To avoid an obstacle directly in front of it, the ship must begin turning when 12 miles (19 km) away.

Recreational boats include sailboats (top) and inflatable rafts (bottom)

SHIP & BOAT
M O T O R

An outboard motor is a gasoline engine mounted at the stern of a boat. The engine is clamped onto the boat and can be easily removed.

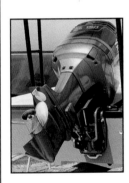

Above, a mounted outboard motor
Right, lake cruising
Far right, boats docked in a calm harbor

Throughout history, the wealth of a country has depended largely on its ability to move cargo along rivers and across oceans. For many centuries before the invention of airplanes, ships were the only way that people could travel from one part of the world to another. Although planes have today largely replaced ships as a means of long-distance travel, there is still something wondrous about riding the waves.

Glossary

Atomic reactors are devices that generate power by breaking down certain elements; they are also called nuclear reactors.

Dugouts are boats made from large logs that have been hollowed out.

The **equator** is the imaginary line that divides the Earth into the Northern Hemisphere and Southern Hemisphere.

Hulls are the outer surfaces of ships that are in contact with the water.

Masts are tall vertical poles that rise from a ship's deck and hold its sails.

Navigators are specially trained sailors who plot a course for a ship to follow.

The **New World** is the name given to North America, South America, and surrounding islands after the voyage of Columbus.

The **Phoenicians** were master sailors of the ancient world who traded throughout the Mediterranean Sea.

Pilgrims were people who sought religious freedom and a better life in the New World.

The **Prime Meridian** is an imaginary north-south line that passes through Greenwich, England.

A **rudder** is a large, flat object that extends below the water and is turned to guide a ship.

Scandinavia is a region that includes the modern countries of Norway, Sweden, and Denmark.

The **stern** is the rear part of a ship; the bow is the front.

The **Strait of Gibraltar** is a 27-mile (43 km) channel that joins the Mediterranean Sea and the Atlantic Ocean.

Trade winds are dependable winds encountered near the equator.

Index